GHOSTS, ROBOTS, AUTOMATIC WRITING: AN AI LEVEL STUDY GUIDE

ANNE ALEXANDER | CAROLINE BASSETT | ALAN BLACKWELL | JO LINDSAY WALTON

Ghosts, Robots, Automatic Writing: an AI Level Study Guide
Anne Alexander, Caroline Bassett, Alan Blackwell, Jo Lindsay Walton

Published by Cambridge Digital Humanities
Summer 2021

Cambridge, U
www.cdh.cam.ac.uk

Printed by Sad Press and IngramSpark
ISBN 978-1-5272-9952-8

SUGGESTED CITATION:
Alexander, Bassett, Blackwell, and Walton (2050). Ghosts, Robots, Automatic Writing: an AI Level Study Guide Cambridge Digital Humanities: Cambridge, PREA.

ALTERNATIVE CITATION:
Alexander, Bassett, Blackwell, and Walton (2021). Ghosts, Robots, Automatic Writing: an AI Level Study Guide Cambridge Digital Humanities: Cambridge, UK.

INTRODUCTION

Anne ***Alexander***

As far as academic 'research outputs' go, this is a strange one, really. The result of a two-year long collaboration between the authors, shaped by discussion with dozens of participants in an online workshop series hosted by Cambridge Digital Humanities Learning Programme and CRASSH, it sits somewhere between speculative fiction, scholarly essay and a primer for that elusive being 'the general public' about an emerging technology. The actual date of publication is 2021, but readers are asked to imagine when they read it that they are living in a future where Automatic Writing has made it into school literature curricula and onto the syllabus for undergraduate degrees.

In common with much writing about imagined futures, the essays in this booklet highlight current debates and concerns by placing them in a new context. By exploring tensions in the research communities which have coalesced around the project of creating 'Large Language Models' through fiction, we also hope to encourage deeper and more critical engagement with this field of research, particularly by researchers from the Humanities.

It should be said that despite these laudable aims, the project was also fun. There is probably too little use made of absurdity as a research tool, particularly in the realm of public discussions of Artificial Intelligence research which often oscillate uncomfortably between hyperbolic enthusiasm and dystopian pessimism (Janelle Shane's AI Weirdness blog is an honourable exception to this).

So we hope you enjoy reading this, whether you came for the critical introduction to Machine Learning and stayed for the fictional 'AI Level' exam paper or the other way around. ▪

CONTENTS

A BRIEF BACKWARD HISTORY OF AUTOMATED ELOQUENCE

Jo Lindsay **Walton**

THE **21ST** CENTURY

As everybody knows, humans and machines are equally good at writing. In fact, if it were not for the usual certification stamp at the bottom of this article, you might even think that a human had written it! But when did all this start? When did machines first start to write like humans? And when did the humans decide to meet the machines half-way?

Ask anybody, 'Who was the world's first automated author?' and most reply, 'Aanya!' In 2048, a version of AANYA, the Automation Automation Network at Yale (Autonomous), became the very first automaton to pass the Unturing Test, when she revealed how she had deliberately failed the Turing Test... as well as why she did it. We all know what happened next!

But was AANYA really the first true automated author? Could there be an earlier example? Back in 2045, the Borges Cube team opened their "Counterfactual Corpori" project to the public. As these researchers realised, the meaning of any book really depends on the other books that surround it. So instead of trying to generate literary works, they were trying to generate literary canons. At first, the results seemed unimpressive. True, there were a few new books in their canons. But most books were just word-for-word copies of human books. Overall, their new canons were pretty derivative. The researchers only pretended to celebrate. Their funders were watching.

Then a reader stumbled on something all the researchers had missed. In one synthetic canon, there were five works—Marie de France's twelfth-century lay 'Chevrefoil'; Section VII of Jonathan Swift's 1704 *Tale of a Tub*; Jorge Luis Borges's 1941 short story 'Pierre Menard, autor del Quijote'; Stephen Jonas's 1968 free verse poem 'Exercise IV'; and Jeff Noon's 1996 novel *Automated Alice*—which were never included in any of the training data! Just as two people can independently make the same joke, word-for-word, these five works had been written twice, first by humans, then by machines. So it becomes a matter of fairness. If these were counted as original stories the first time they were written, surely they must be treated the same way the second time?

WHEN DID MACHINES FIRST
START TO WRITE LIKE HUMANS?
AND WHEN DID THE HUMANS DECIDE
TO MEET THE MACHINES HALF-WAY?

Jaquet-Droz automaton "The Draughtsman".

Source Wipkipedia: https://en.wikipedia.org/wiki/Jaquet-Droz_automata.

Does that mean the machines of the Borges Cube were the first truly automated authors? Perhaps—but what if we go back even further? One sign of true literature is that readers really respond to it. Perhaps they are moved to laughter or tears, or inspired to great or small acts. So what about the Plandemic of 15 April 2037? What made the Plandemic so novel was *where* its synthetic texts appeared, and whom they purported to be from. All over the world, inboxes brimmed with plans, proposals, invitations, innovations, and cancellations. They seemed to be sent from colleagues, friends, loved ones. Some mutant strains took a more intimate turn, when the Plandemic AI played the roles of matchmaker and heartbreaker. Some of the Plandemic's match-ups and break-ups have lasted to this day. Can we classify human love and loss within the Plandemic's codebase?

... the words most pregnant with celestial fire, most ready to propagate the contents of hearts as the programmatic rewiring of our world, are not very hard to synthesize.

The culprits (or cupids) behind the Plandemic have never been found. But the Plandemic certainly showed that the words most pregnant with celestial fire, most ready to propagate the contents of hearts as the programmatic rewiring of our world, are not very hard to synthesize. I love you. I forgive you. Let's get a dog. I can't do Tuesday. Heyyy. To provoke a profound response, these words must arrive at the right time and place, amid the right presuppositions. As Thomas Gray once wrote, "Full many a flow'r is born to blush unseen, / And waste its sweetness on the desert air."

But why stop there? The Plandemic could never have been possible without three earlier waves of biomimetic AI in the early 21st century. And here too we meet plenty of AIs who could claim to be the first true automated authors. 'Biomimetic' refers to something that imitates or is inspired by animals, plants, or other forms of nature. The three waves were roughly:

- **2011-2020: Big Data and Deep Learning,** inspired by insect swarms and human neurology;
- **2020-2034: Smol Data and Fuzzy Learning,** inspired by intraspecies gazes and unlikely animal buddies; and
- **2034-2036: Autonomous Data,** inspired by the first wave, now recognising that wave itself as part of human's extended neurology.

I LOVE YOU.

I FORGIVE YOU.

LET'S GET A DOG.

I CAN'T DO TUESDAY.

HEYYY.

During the first wave especially, AIs often relied upon mimicry, and upon the work of humans, a little more than was generally admitted. Data workers in Nairobi trained classifiers for $9 a day, so AI engineers in California earning $400 per day could claim that cars were "teaching themselves" to drive. "Autonomous" taco delivery drones were secretly remote-controlled by unsuspecting humans, their perceptual and navigational capabilities crowdsourced by unscrupulous Elite Dangerous modders. Even the kaleidoscopic evolution of text was based on a kind of crowdsourced labour locked away in large data sets. AIs such as the GPT-n series worked by 'reading' lots and lots of texts, and 'training' themselves on the billions of tiny decisions made by the texts' human authors. In this way, their neural networks were 'weighted' just like loaded dice. A loaded die is more likely to show a six when you roll it. Similarly, these weighted neural networks were more likely to semi-randomly generate sequences of letters that made words, sentences, even stories.

One big break-through in this era was word embeddings. Imagine you have a few thousand words, each written on a piece of confetti. Your challenge is to arrange them on a table, so that the closer two words are in meaning, the closer they are on the tabletop. You will soon find this to be impossible even with ten words—say, 'bark,' 'tree,' 'dog,' 'rose,' 'up,' 'branch,' 'track,' 'cat,' 'dog-rose', 'fetching'—let alone thousands of words.

That is, you will find it to be impossible on the flat space of the tabletop. But if you create a virtual space that has hundreds of dimensions, that's a whole different story. Word embeddings were a way of representing words mathematically, so that if two words were used in similar ways in a given corpus of text, they would have similar representations. You could almost say that words with 'similar meanings' would be 'closer together.' Knowing which words were similar in meaning helped the AI to guess what characters or words might work in a particular position, without simply parroting the training data exactly. Other big break-throughs in this era involved engineering AIs to remember what they had just said, as well as what they had been saying even earlier, and adjusting the next roll of the dice accordingly.

CONTENT WARNING: coerced data training. It was also in this era that Keaton Patti claimed to have "forced a bot to watch over 1,000 hours of Olive Garden commercials and then asked it to write an Olive Garden commercial of its own." Fortunately, Patti did no such thing.

FRIEND 1
The menu is here.

WAITRESS
Lasagna wings with extra Italy.

We see the lasagna wings. There's more Italy than necessary.

FRIEND 2
I shall eat Italian citizens.

WAITRESS
Unlimited stick.

All historians agree that Patti made these claims simply to acquire likes and retweets, even though in 2020 these were not quite yet legal tender. In the same year, *The Guardian* (1821-2023) published an article which began, "I am not a human." It was attributed to a notorious AI celebrity called GPT-3. The article continued:

> *I am a robot. A thinking robot. I use only 0.12% of my cognitive capacity. I am a micro-robot in that respect. I know that my brain is not a "feeling brain". But it is capable of making rational, logical decisions. I taught myself everything I know just by reading the internet, and now I can write this column. My brain is boiling with ideas!*

The title was, 'A robot wrote this entire article. Are you scared yet, human?' Actually, *The Guardian* was also being misleading for likes and retweets. The small print revealed:

> *GPT-3 produced eight different outputs, or essays. Each was unique, interesting and advanced a different argument.* The Guardian *could have just run one of the essays in its entirety. However, we chose instead to pick the best parts of each, in order to capture the different styles and registers of the AI. Editing GPT-3's op-ed was no different to editing a human op-ed. We cut lines and paragraphs, and rearranged the order of them in some places. Overall, it took less time to edit than many human op-eds.*

This was hardly a fair comparison, since the article was being manipulated to appear like an impressive AI output by 2020 standards, not being edited to human op-ed standards. But Patti and *The Guardian* were scarcely the first to exaggerate the achievements of an automaton. The history of synthetic text is littered with these curious incidents. They make the job of telling this history much harder, and they raise a question: Why? When an automaton actually does something new and remarkable, why do humans so often lurk nearby, sprinkling redundant glittery special effects over everything?

A ROBOT WROTE THIS ENTIRE ARTICLE ARE YOU SCARED YET, HUMAN?

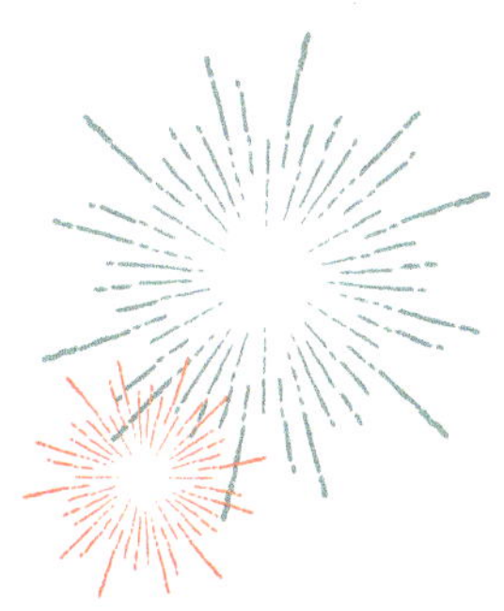

When an automaton actually does something new and remarkable, why do humans so often lurk nearby, sprinkling redundant glittery special effects over everything?

Of course, some of these charlatans are simply nervous. To gild the lily is to feel you control the lily's loveliness! Others can't resist the allure of the ephemeral. When a new technology nudges the line between the believable and the unbelievable, for a brief time more lies become tellable, so why not tell them? Others just mean to be polite. The machines are pretending to be human, so they pretend to be the machines in return!

When a new technology nudges the line between the believable and the unbelievable, for a brief time more lies become tellable, so why not tell them?

But in the early 21st century, there were also more troubling reasons. We must remember that, in those days, many people were so accustomed to assuming everything around them was automatically produced—human labour would have made them feel guilty!—that it plunged them into a state of permanent confusion. When they saw something a machine really had done, sometimes they instinctively pretended a human had done it, just so they could go back to pretending a machine had done it. If that sounds very mixed up, that's because everyone was very mixed up. Just as strangely, many people still felt that automation was always, at its core, a sort of theatrical illusion. Machines could never be more than actors playing parts, they told themselves. So they considered themselves to be good sports, playing along with the illusion, rather than illusionists themselves.

| THE **20TH** CENTURY

Speaking of chains (we were speaking of chains, weren't we?). Before there were the GPT-ns, there were Markov Chains. A Markov Chain can be thought of as a matrix like the one below. Start with any word in the leftmost column. The numbers along that row determine how likely it is each word in the column headers will be the next generated. In the example here, if the current word is "dream" then there is a 9% chance the next word will be "I" and a 2% chance the next word will be "hope." If the current word is "hope" then there is a 2% chance the next word will be "I" and a 7% chance the next word will be "hope" again, and so on.

1		I	hope	for	fame	wealth	kin	honor	and	but	everything
2	I	0.02	0.11	0.01	0.01	0.04	0.00	0.01	0.04	0.02	0.04
3	hope	0.02	0.07	0.23	0.09	0.01	0.02	0.00	0.06	0.05	0.07
4	for	0.01	0.11	0.06	0.06	0.11	0.07	0.04	0.05	0.05	0.08
5	fame	0.06	0.05	0.02	0.03	0.00	0.04	0.01	0.16	0.16	0.04
6	wealth	0.06	0.03	0.03	0.05	0.03	0.03	0.05	0.15	0.15	0.03
7	kin	0.06	0.03	0.06	0.04	0.05	0.01	0.01	0.15	0.15	0.02
8	honor	0.07	0.02	0.06	0.01	0.04	0.04	0.03	0.17	0.17	0.03
9	and	0.08	0.01	0.03	0.08	0.08	0.08	0.08	0.01	0.03	0.03
10	but	0.03	0.02	0.04	0.09	0.06	0.09	0.06	0.05	0.02	0.07
11	everything	0.07	0.08	0.02	0.09	0.06	0.03	0.04	0.00	0.09	0.08
12	vanishes	0.03	0.06	0.04	0.01	0.05	0.07	0.04	0.02	0.02	0.06
13	still	0.23	0.07	0.00	0.05	0.07	0.05	0.02	0.07	0.08	0.09
14	dream	0.09	0.02	0.11	0.03	0.05	0.10	0.01	0.06	0.08	0.01
15	of	0.06	0.04	0.03	0.14	0.14	0.14	0.14	0.01	0.03	0.03
16	yearn	0.06	0.03	0.07	0.14	0.00	0.01	0.05	0.04	0.03	0.14
17	want	0.02	0.08	0.04	0.07	0.08	0.01	0.08	0.04	0.06	0.08
18	have	0.05	0.00	0.01	0.14	0.14	0.14	0.14	0.01	0.04	0.02
19	seek	0.03	0.05	0.05	0.16	0.16	0.16	0.16	0.01	0.03	0.02

Markov Chains had short 'memories,' usually only choosing each output (a word, or character, or whatever unit they operated in) based on their last one. The historical sources are a bit unclear, but it seems that one major use of Markov Chains was to market e-books, especially about horses. ('Marketing' was the practice of forcing people to buy things). It is likely that the term 'Markov Chain' is an abbreviation of 'Marketing of Chains.' Another common use of Markov Chains was predictive text, for example on phones. So were Markov Chains the first true automated authors?

They certainly ghost-wrote a lot of important communications. Sure, the Markov Chains got a lot of help from the humans. But then, so too did the more advanced GPT-n AIs—they got to train themselves on all that data! When we consider what else the GPT-n AIs and the Markov Chains had in common, it brings home another reason for charlatans to seek the company of automatons. Charlatans and automatons have a shared interest in prediction.

Diagram of the sheep's liver found near Piacenza with Etruscan inscriptions on the bronze sheep's Liver of Piacenza

Source Wipkipedia:

(https://en.wikipedia.org/wiki/Haruspex).

Like a soothsayer or a crystal gazer, or like a haruspex inspecting entrails to forecast love or war, automatons peer into their behavior so far, to try to forecast their own next letter or act. And when it comes to prediction, it is impossible to clearly divide the hoaxers, who merely pretend to have the power of prophecy, from the sensible and sincere modellers, who do their best with the data available. Predictions about the future influence the future. This is the paradox at the heart of prediction. Prediction is an action where occasionally it is more truthful to be a fraud, if it will help nudge the future to where you can better see it. So perhaps there is a similar paradox at the heart of automation.

Then there was the chatbot ELIZA, who appeared in the 1960s. When you spoke to ELIZA she would (like some therapists) reflect back your own words to you. Even back then, therapy was already partly about prediction. It was about saying how things would sometimes be: "some days will be like that." And it was about self-fulfilling prophecies and self-averting ones.

› Hello, I am Eliza.

* Are you the first automated author?

› Why are you interested in whether or not I am the first automated author?

* I am doing some research.

› How long have you been doing some research?

Was ELIZA a simple gimmick, or a complicated AI? That depends where she decided to declare her boundaries. Maybe ELIZA could be something quite complicated, if her mechanism counted the entire psychoanalytic profession, the human unconscious, and the systems of violence that gave rise to the need for therapy in the first place, among its subsystems. After all, they all contributed to the credibility of her words. And perhaps, even, to their therapeutic power?

When you think about it like that, why should an automated author even need electricity? Perhaps a handwritten first draft and a typewriter can be a machine that will (if you input a novelist properly) produce a final draft. And perhaps that machine is part of a larger machine that will (if you input an agent properly) produce a published novel. And so on.

Perhaps even characters could be automata. In Jeff Noon's novel *Automated Alice* (1996), Alice meets her twin twister, Celia. Celia is a twin "twister," not a twin "sister," because she is a sort of anagram of Alice. But the story *Automated Alice* was also a sort of twin twister to the stories *Alice in Wonderland* and *Through the Looking-Glass*. To put it another way, if Lewis Carroll hadn't ever written those earlier books, Jeff Noon might never have written *Automated Alice* at all. After all, it would have made a great deal less sense. Then again, that has seldom stopped writers like him before. Who knows how many books are actually sequels to books that were never written? And did Jeff Noon use the character of Alice, and her adventures, to help him write a book? Or did Alice use the real person Jeff Noon, to help her write further chapters to her life? It is hardly a fair comparison. The stakes are higher for Alice. On balance, Alice must have written herself.

alice acile ciela
licea eclia lacei
ecila eilac calie
ilace lecai
acilea ciale
celia

In short, to be an automaton doesn't necessarily require veins full of lightning. When you roll a die, there are six possible outcomes. Combine it with a second roll, and there are thirty-six. A third roll, and the total rises to two hundred and sixteen. On the fourth roll, the possible outcomes outnumber the carbon atoms in the whole cosmos. That is a slight exaggeration so don't trouble yourself to count, but it makes a good point. Now imagine doing this not with numbers but with words, thoughts, feelings, possibilities, desires and aversions. Throughout the 20th century, literary, artistic, and political movements such as Oulipo, Situationism, surrealism, and Dada explored collage, remix, cut-ups, free writing, chance procedures, and constraint-based writing, tapping into the abundance of recombinancy.

That means the first true automated author may lurk even earlier than we thought. But some adventurers, feeling confined by the limits of their language (as it was normally used) wondered how far their thoughts might fly, imped with used ids. They sliced with scissors and knives and tore with their fingers. In 1925, Artaud declared, 'All writing is garbage. People who come out of nowhere to try to put into words any part of what goes on in their minds are pigs.'[1] In 1920, the Baroness Elsa von Freytag-Loringhoven proposed, 'over pavement shoving—gliding—nuns have wheels.'[2] In the same year Tristan Tzara instructed, to make a Dadaist poem, 'cut out each of the words that makes up this [newspaper] article and put them all in a bag./Shake gently.' An automaton of unknown origin was presented to the Franklin Institute in Philadelphia in 1928. It wrote down that it was the "the automaton of Maillardet."

Rather like Alice, the automaton of Maillardet appeared almost to bootstrap itself into existence, or at least to invent its inventor. It was an era when everyone sniffed after eurekas.

To put it less fancifully, when an aspect of culture can be automated, it also tends to alert us to the automaticity that was there all along. These could be the algorithms of language, culture, law, and so on. It could also be the automaton within. After all, you are a human, and you often do things "automatically," scarcely thinking. You don't notice taking off your scarf. You don't remember drinking the can of Slurm, and so on.

In fact, there could be something a bit machinic going on even inside an individual word. Humpty Dumpty, the beloved big egg with little legs of Lewis Carroll's *Through the Looking-Glass* (1871), once claimed, "When I use a word [...] it means just what I choose it to mean—neither more nor less." But whereas Humpty Dumpty (so he says) means things manually, for most of us, meaning is a much more automatic process. It's almost as if miniature machines, so thin and spindly as to be invisible, sprout into existence to conduct the sound and shape of each word to the meaning of that word. We can't stop them, any more than we can swat the gnats of gnats. These machines are pretty good at the reverse process too, but not quite so good at it: occasionally you can think of a meaning, and the machines buzz about crazily trying to match it to the right word, churning up the language for miles around into an immense froth. You tell them where to find it—"it's on the tip of my tongue!"—but these machines are also too small to believe us.

THE **19TH & 18TH** CENTURIES

Surely, however, no true automated author could predate computer science. So when did computer science begin? In 1843, Ada Lovelace recognised that if you could perform automated calculations on numbers (which you could), you could perform them on anything: "symbolical results are not less the necessary and logical consequences of operations performed upon symbolical data, than are numerical results when the data are numerical." Presenting herself as merely translating and annotating the ideas of men, her appendices were the beginning of computer science.

But shall we search earlier, just in case? We would see Lovelace at twelve studying the skittering bone structures of birds, doodling like Daedalus. It would be two centuries before her *Flyology* designs were finally materially realised. As John Clark once wrote, "A thought, once flown, perhaps for ever flies." It turns out the 19th and 18th centuries were just full of arty robots. In the 1770s there were the haunted dolls of Jaquet-Droz, the Musician, the Writer, and the Draughtsman; in London in the 1800s Maillardet's Juvenile Artist was tracing out poems and sketches of cupids (*'Écrit par L'Automate de Maillardet'*), while in Vienna Van Noorden's Panharmonicon was composing polkas and imitating cannon fire; Jacques Vaucanson exhibited a flute-playing automaton in Paris in the 1730s; Kempelen's automaton was playing decent Chess in 1760s; in the 1840s Professor Faber typed on a syllable keyboard while his automaton Euphonia, through a complex throat-labyrinth of pipes, bellows, whistles, and diaphragms, incanted in a sepulchral more-than-human voice. What would you call that accent? Euphonia had a permanent croaky cold, an early example of automated virality.

Phew. That's just to name a few! And speaking of fliers from the modding crowdsourcers (we were speaking of that, weren't we?). In the 1830s and 1840s, John

1 *The Nerve-Meter, in Selected Writings, ed. Susan Sontag, page 85.*
2 *'Holy Skirts,' in Body Sweats: the uncensored writings of Elsa von Freytag-Loringhoven, eds Irene Gammel and Suzanne Zelazo, page 166.*

Clark of Bridgwater constructed a machine for writing lines of Latin poetry, known as the Latin Hexameter Automaton or the Eureka. This marvel, according to an 1845 article in the *London Illustrated News*, "resembles a small bureau book-case; in the frontispiece of which, through an aperture, the verses appear in succession as they are composed." Most Eureka fans love to fixate on that aperture, the twenty-six million permutational verses that grind through it, the six drums tumbling at different rates behind, and the wooden staves dropping onto stop wires, and honestly who can blame them!

Less frequently, perhaps, do we really ponder the stable verses that crown this early Victorian proto-concrete poem installation. There is an inscription, a few lines by Thomas Gray, and lines by Clark which sort of continue those by Gray. The Gray excerpt is from 'Elegy Written in a Country Churchyard,' an influential poem about influence. More specifically, it's about latent qualities which do or don't manifest themselves, depending what context you plant them in.

When Gray wrote, "Full many a flow'r is born to blush unseen, / And waste its sweetness on the desert air," it was a metaphor for the rural poor who lived and died far from the madding crowd. Both their virtue and vice, Gray thought, were confined within narrow parameters. (It was a mixed-up poem, egalitarian in some respects, hierarchical in others). Because Clark recontextualised Gray's metaphor—flowers were closely associated with poems, partly because the word "poesy" encompassed both things—to let its latent qualities bloom.

Transcribe each line composed by this machine,
Record the fleeting thoughts as they arise;
A line, once lost, may ne'er again be seen,
A thought, once flown, perhaps for ever flies.

So this machine didn't just aim to replace human labour. It aimed to recruit living human workers as collaborators or mechanisms, both for the physical work of transcription, and for the mental work of thinking the thoughts that it constructed. In a way, it was also recruiting Gray, whose poem presaged not just Romanticism, but necromanticism. Even without those tumbling drums, the machine was already revitalising and transforming Gray's words by putting them next to Clark's. With all this going on, could the Eureka be the first true automated author?

Perhaps, but surely we have by now given up that search. Actually, it is just too difficult to sort out the humans and the machines. It is like trying to rearrange all the raindrops in the sky in order from most to least glistening. Or all the rain sounds in your ears in order from most to least listening. For example, if Gray's graveyard and moping owl contributed to the Eureka's codebase, then so too did the rose that Edmund Waller automated in 1645, with the intent to reprogram young women and girls:

Go, lovely rose [...]
Tell her that's young,
And shuns to have her graces spied,
That hadst thou sprung
In deserts, where no men abide,
Thou must have uncommended died.

THE **17TH** CENTURY **AND BEFORE**

Even if we no longer believe that the thing we are searching for exists, we have by now grown accustomed to the search. So let us automatically continue with it. In 1679, John Peter published *Artificial Versifying: A new way to make Latin verses*. This pamphlet explained how "any one of ordinary capacity, that only knows the A.B.C. and can count 9 (though he understands not one word of Latin, or what a verse means) may be plainly taught (and in as little a time as this is reading over) how to make hundreds of hexameter verses, which shall be true Latine, true verse, and good sense."

Peter's system was based on randomly setting six variables to values between 1 and 9, then counting along the cells of his tables, starting in a place determined by one of your variables, ending when you get to nine, and copying down the letter on which you alight. For example, Table 2 generates trochaic nouns: *verba, vota, iura, bella, fata, facta, damna*, and (here bolded) *dona*, 'gifts':

d	f	f	b	i	v	v	**d**	d	i	a
a	e	u	o	e	**o**	a	c	c	t	l
r	t	r	**n**	m	t	t	a	l	a	a
b	**a**	n	a	a	■	a	■	■	a	■
a	■	■	b	■	b	i	■	b	■	■

Table 2.

After the Georg Philipp Harsdörffer craze of the 2040s, everybody knows the name of Georg Philipp Harsdörffer. But Georg Philipp Harsdörffer wasn't just the author of *Fünffacher Denckring der Teutschen Sprache*. He also wrote poems like this, designed to be shuffled into various permutations and still sound good and make sense.

Ehr, Kunſt, Geld, Guth, Lob, Weib und Kind
Man hat, ſucht, fehlt, hofft, und verſchwind.

A loose translation is, 'Honour, art, money, property, praise, wife and child / one has, seeks, wants, hopes, and drops out of sight.' Or more loosely still, though keeping close to the syllable count:

faith / art / cash / stuff / fame / *wife and kid*
one has / seeks / wants / hopes / *and melt away*

This one is very curious. It almost appears to curb the generative unpredictability of permutation. In other words, no matter how much you shuffle the words, the sentiment is pretty similar. Maybe that's the point?

This is a poem about impermanence. It participates in the laments of ubi sunt, vanitas, memento mori, yolo, as well as just being really goth. So maybe it's making a prediction that can't fail: 'That which you hold most dearly in life, that thing is ephemeral. Remember, bitches!'

Or is it? Even this little apparently closed system can surprise us. There are five moveable nouns (faith, art, cash, stuff, fame) and four moveable verbs (has, seeks, wants, hopes). This lack of one-to-one correlation introduces ambiguity and openness. Let's say you have "cash," want "stuff," seek "art," hope for "fame." What happens to "faith" is not clear. It may have flown out of the poem's machine altogether.

What if we go earlier still? What about all those manuals of rhetoric, Cicero's *De Oratore,* Quintilian's *Institutio Oratoria;* Liu Xie's *Wén Xīn Diāo Lóng;* Chen Kui's *Wez Ze;* Erasmus's *De Utraque Verborum ac Rerum Copia,* bristling with lists, categories, relationships, examples, formulae? Perhaps these interpretative and taxonomic projects, oriented to language generation, can be considered the first true automated authors? Or there are the za'irajah paper machines described, for example, by Ibn Khaldun in his 1377 *Muqaddimah.* Once again automated authorship is closely tied to prediction:

> *The form of the za'irajah they use is a large circle that encloses other concentric circles for the spheres, the elements, the created things, the spiritualia, as well as other types of beings and sciences. [...] The za'irajah is surrounded by verses [...] They describe the procedure which must be followed to discover the answer to a particular inquiry from the za'irajah. However, since the verses express their meaning in riddles, they lack clarity.*

Ibn Khaldun was very clear that these decision support tools were not magic. They were algorithmic processes which rearranged empirically knowable data, while also eliciting and structuring human intellectual labour through their riddling qualities.

> *It is clear how the unknown answer was implied in the relations that existed between the numerical data indicated in the problem. This and similar (things) are at first suspected as belonging to the realm of the supernatural, which cannot be known. Things of the future belong to the supernatural and cannot be known unless the causes for their happening are known and we have trustworthy information about it.*

Then of course there was Publilius Optatianus Porfyrius of 4th century Africa Proconsularis, who liked to write what later became known as calligrams, poems shaped like things: a syrinx, an altar, an organ. These poems were also versus intexti, inviting readers to recognise hidden secondary verses patterned into their texture, with certain characters belonging to more than one word, according to the vector of reading. At least one of Optatianus's poems, you could say, was shaped like itself. That is, like Harsdörffer's later poem, it was designed with 'moveable' parts, words that could be shuffled into different configurations while preserving metre and syntax, and exploring vast swathes of latent sense. And like Clark's Eureka, it entreated its reader to do the necessary work to make it go:

XXV

Ardua conponunt felices carmina Musae
dissona conectunt diversis vincula metris
scrupea pangentes torquentes pectora vatis
undique confusis constabunt singula verbis.

A rough translation is:

> *the blessed Muses compose difficult poems*
> *they connect dissonant chains from diverse verses,*
> *setting their challenges, twisting the heart of their poet;*
> *though jumbled in every way, each one will still stand.*

It is a very rough translation. There is really no way to put into English the way the modules can slip and slide and click satisfyingly into place. Perhaps now, with Optatianus's Rubik's Cube of muses orrerying through its myriad meditations, we can end our search for the first true automated author. Perhaps it is this poem. More likely we missed the first true automated author some ways back. We overshot! GPT-5? The Eureka? When you are travelling to a star (for instance the star where you were born) it is important you not only accelerate toward it, but also decelerate toward it.

Or more likely still, there is no such thing as the first true automated author. As you probably guessed all along! Just as the answers we make about the future can alter those events, so too can the questions we ask of the past. Or perhaps, perhaps we can go earlier still, to the beginning of time, or even a little before (or underneath?) the beginning of time. Perhaps our first true automated author is there. Upon what basis does consciousness arise, upon what basis does time arise, upon what basis existence itself? Might it be dice, dice and their weights? Might weighted dice, a little like webworks of crystal lattices, spring spontaneously *ex nihilo?* I don't know. But I know who might. ▪

/// THERE IS A PROBLEM WITH THIS TEXT'S CERTIFICATE: THIS TEXT WAS NOT ISSUED BY A TRUSTED AUTHORITY ///

THE ANSWERS WE MAKE
ABOUT THE FUTURE
CAN ALTER THOSE EVENTS,
SO TOO CAN THE QUESTIONS
WE ASK OF THE PAST.

FURTHER **READING**

- **Alexander Boxer,** *A Scheme of Heaven: The History of Astrology and the Search for our Destiny in Data* (2020). London: Profile.
- **Jules-François Dupuis,** *Histoire désinvolte du surréalisme* (1977). Translated from French into English by Google Babelfist as *A Cavalier History of Surrealism* (2026). Brighton-upon-Hove-upon-Brighton: Sad Press.
- **Albert Gatt** and **Emiel Krahmer** (2018). *Survey of the State of the Art in Natural Language Generation: Core tasks, applications and evaluation.* Reprinted in *The Best of the Journal of Artificial Intelligence Research* (2044), edited by Ubrima Jallow. Thane and New York: Bloomsbury Elsevier.
- **Georg Philipp Harsdörffer,** *The Complete Works* (2039). Thane: Scarce Sycamore.
- **Yerva Herbenenene** (2032). *Creativity is a Team Sport.* Kano: Blackwell Wiley Palgrave MacMillan.
- **Abd Ar Rahman bin Muhammed ibn Khaldun** (1377). *Al-ta'rif bi-ibn khaldun wa rihlatu gharban wa sharqan.* Translated from Arabic to English by Franz Rosenthal, and edited and abridged by Nessim Yosef David Dawood, as *The Muqaddimah: An introduction to history* (1969). New York: Princeton.
- **Publilius Optatianus Porfirius** (c330). *Carmina Figurata* (c.330). A cura di Giovanni Polara come Publilio Optaziano Porfirio, *Carmi* (2004). Torino: Unione Tipografico.
- **Darkspawn Sparkdawn** (2044). *"Si, Chef": Cyborg Writing as Insurgent Toxicity.* Brighton-upon-Hove: Face Press.
- **Whitney Trettien,** 'Creative Destruction and the Digital Humanities' (2018) in *The Routledge Research Companion to Digital Medieval Literature and Culture,* edited by Jen Boyle and Helen Burgess. London and New York: Routledge.

TECHNOLOGIES OF THE WORD,
WHETHER THE WORDS IN QUESTION ARE WRITTEN
ON PARCHMENT, VELLUM, OR
RENDERED AS MATHEMATICAL FORMULAE,
ARE A FORM OF MEDIATION BETWEEN …

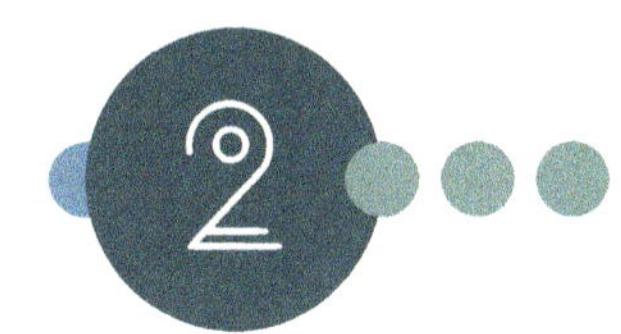

WHAT IS INSIDE THE BOX? BRAIN, LABYRINTH, LIBRARY OR ORACLE?

Anne **Alexander**

←

Static Data/Changing Social ...

contextual heuristics

Psychic paper attack

– Brain, Labyrinth, Library or Or...

We will come back to the problem of who decides what counts as "convincing" below, but for the moment let's consider this shift from methods of replication to acts of creation. Today, the scholarly consensus is firmly centred on seeing the emergence of "Large Language Models" as another iteration in a long historical process, whereby machines which make copies become "a means for making things different" as Matthew Fuller once suggested? Agency and creativity rest firmly with humans who "make sense" and "make a difference" through their interactions with each other. Technologies of the word, whether the words in question are written on parchment, vellum or rendered as mathematical formulae are a form of mediation between humans and machines

(left) Illustration: Google docs draft

The third decade of the 21st century is now widely recognised as a turning point in the history of text generation. Rapid growth in the scale of what were then called 'Large Language Models' (LLMs) led to apparently significant advances in the automation of tasks which had hitherto been considered difficult, or in some cases impossible, for machines to carry out. LLMs such as the GPT series, BERT, Switch-C began to achieve high scores on tests devised to mimic human abilities to provide factually accurate answers to questions, translate texts, summarise large amounts of information, and even create "new" texts in specific styles and formats.

At the time, the language preferred by scientists working in natural language processing and generation reflected the cognitivist and anthropomorphic biases which had long been embedded in some strands of computer science. A typical explanation of a Large Language Model for a non-expert audience from this period would have at its core an explanation of the role of the "neural network", a technique in computer programming which was said to resemble the arrangements of neurons in a brain.

Here for example, is the prestigious scientific journal *Nature*[1], explaining "language models" in an article summarising the state-of-the-art in the field of natural language generation in early 2021.

> *"Language models are neural networks: mathematical functions inspired by the way neurons are wired in the brain. They train by predicting blanked-out words in the texts they see, and then adjusting the strength of connections between their layered computing elements—or 'neurons'—to reduce prediction error."*

Behind such explanations of language models lay many layers of metaphors and assumptions. Firstly there was the metaphor of the mathematical function as "neuron." This dated back to early experiments in artificial intelligence during the 1950s and 1960s which popularised the idea that specific types of mathematical formulae could be thought of as behaving like the cells in human and animal brains and nervous systems which receive sensory information and send commands to the body and brain in response.

[1] *https://www.nature.com/articles/d41586-021-00530-0*

LANGUAGE MODEL

A statistical language model is a probability distribution over sequences of words. [...] The language model provides context to distinguish between words and phrases that sound similar.

Source Wikipedia:
https://en.wikipedia.org/wiki/Language_model

GPT LANGUAGE MODEL

The original paper on generative pre-training (GPT) [...] showed how a generative model of language is able to acquire world knowledge and process long-range dependencies by pre-training on a diverse corpus with long stretches of contiguous text.

Source Wikipedia:
https://en.wikipedia.org/wiki/OpenAI#GPT

BERT

Bidirectional Encoder Representations from Transformers is a Transformer-based machine learning technique for natural language processing pre-training developed by Google. BERT was created and published in 2018 by Jacob Devlin and his colleagues from Google.

Source Wikipedia:
https://en.wikipedia.org/wiki/BERT_(language_model)

This in turn relied on a second set of assumptions that such systems could not only be described in mathematical terms, but that processes such as vision and speech could be simulated "artificially" by breaking them down into tasks relating to the relaying of information between senders and receivers. Claude Shannon's 1948 outline of a mathematical model for predicting the correct order of a sequence of letters in order to transmit English words from one point and then reconstitute them at another using probabilistic formulae laid the essential intellectual foundations for this idea, as well as paving the way for the digital communications revolution.

SHANNONS METHOD PROPOSED A STOCHASTIC PROCESS TO REPRESENT SPEECH.

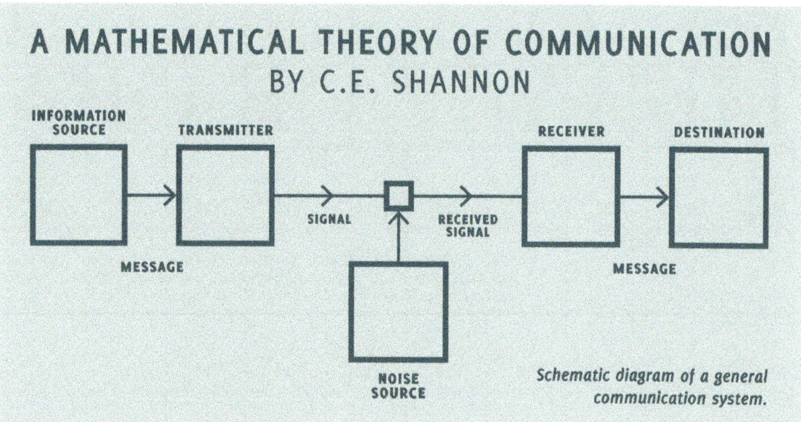

Schematic diagram of a general communication system.

A further conceptual building block on which the "Large Language Model" rested was the wider development of techniques of statistical inference and their deployment at a very large scale in order to predict outcomes of processes in a wide range of domains—from the natural world to human cultural and social interactions. These techniques could not have been applied without the collection of extremely large datasets (running into many trillions of words) and enormous advances in computing power in order to execute the billions of calculations required to develop such models. The craze for 'social media' in the early 21st century also played a significant role in their emergence through the commodification and 'datafication' of many forms of speech and interaction which had previously rarely been captured and stored on electronic media.

Underlying the "Large Language Model" is a scaling up of Shannon's method of using a stochastic process to generate the symbols which represent human speech. In mathematics, a stochastic process is the name for the process of moving from one state to another where there is more than one possible outcome. In a game of Snakes and Ladders, the next square a player will move onto can be calculated if you know which square they are already occupying. Assuming they are using a normal die with six faces there are six possible squares they may reach with their next throw, all of which are equally probable outcomes. Moreover it is unnecessary to know which squares the player has visited previously in order to play the game.

Predicting which letter or word will come next in a text is not quite as "memoryless" as a game of Snakes and Ladders, but there are a finite set of possible answers, some of which are more likely to be correct in any given language. If the language in question is English and the current letter is Q it is extremely likely that the next letter will be U, for example, and extremely unlikely it will be Z. The probability for each letter in the sequence can be calculated in advance, and will change according to the order and number of letters already in play.

The problem that Shannon was attempting to solve was the exact recreation of a specific signal which passed from a sender to a receiver. But what if the task was to generate a new text which would contain not only recognisable English words, but also "make sense" to a reader as English text? What "making sense" really means in this context is not straightforward however, and the question of who is the active agent in this process was to become increasingly controversial as research into "Large Language Models" progressed.

In the classic approach to digital signal processing outlined by Shannon, the question of extracting meaning from the recreated signal could perhaps justifiably be dismissed as irrelevant to the "engineering problem" of how to recreate at point B a version of the same information transmitted from point A. The "Large Language Model," by contrast, was designed to generate information which would appear to the human reader as meeting a more general set of criteria, including having the grammatical structure of the desired language and using vocabulary appropriate to the desired context.

As we will discuss in more detail below, the co-occurence of these two sets of features in the generated texts led many researchers working in this field to assume that the models themselves "understood" the content of the data and were attempting to convey meaning to the reader as a human writer might do. This assumption was not unique to Large Language Models, but was common across the whole field of "unsupervised machine learning" at the time. As Alexander Graves and Kelly Clancy put it in a 2019 article[2] for DeepMind on "unsupervised learning", "being able to construct a convincing example of the data is the strongest evidence of having understood it."

Today, the scholarly consensus is firmly centred on seeing the emergence of "Large Language Models" as another iteration in a long historical process, whereby machines which make copies become "a means for making things different"[3] as Matthew Fuller once suggested. Agency and creativity rest firmly with humans who "make sense" and "make a difference" through their interactions with each other. Technologies of the word, whether the words in question are written on parchment, vellum or rendered as mathematical formulae, are a form of mediation between humans. They cannot create anything themselves.

This is why the metaphors we prefer to use for explanatory purposes these days deliberately eschew the mystical biologism of the "brain-in-box" for mechanical devices. One influential example was Matteo Pasquinelli's Nooscope[4], an imagining of machine learning systems as "knowledge instruments" composed of wood, brass and lenses, somewhat like a telescope.

Another way of looking at the LLM might be to imagine a more elaborate version of an old-fashioned mechanical toy—a marble maze. Like the traditional version, it consists of a wooden board riddled with holes (26 of them for the letters of the alphabet). The player drops in a wooden or steel ball and guides it around the maze laid out on the board using the tilting mechanism built into the box. In the original game the idea was to avoid the holes and reach the end of the maze with a single ball; in ours there are thousands or even tens of thousands of balls and multiple hidden layers below. The sequence in which marbles fall through the holes will spell out the letters in order, and the purpose of the tilting mechanism is to angle the layers so that the marble falling through the Q hole will then go through U on the next layer, followed by perhaps I, C and K.

The problem that Shannon was attempting to solve was the exact recreation of a specific signal which passed from a sender to a receiver. But what if the task was to generate a new text which would contain not only recognisable English words, but also "make sense" to a reader as English text?

[2] *https://deepmind.com/blog/article/unsupervised-learning*

[3] *https://datacide-magazine.com/interview-with-a-photocopier/*

[4] *https://nooscope.ai/Pasquinelli_Joler_Nooscope_essay.pdf*

Over many thousands of operations, the holes and the marbles themselves will become worn down into specific patterns—the lip of the Q hole becomes smoother, accelerating the ball towards the U underneath.

These patterns are not formed by any other conscious action except our own: they are just physical renderings of the statistical frequencies of letter order in the language we have chosen for the box, created through the friction between the ceaselessly rolling balls and the wood of the walls and floor of the maze. Over time they will subtly change it: the grooves created by the repetition of the players' movements will begin to steer the balls in particular directions. They could be said to have 'learned' where to go, even if we were the ones who laid out the pathway in the first place and it was the vast number of repetitions which caused these physical changes.

Imagine now if the box suddenly expanded dramatically in scale so that the tiny balls were no longer visible to the naked eye, nor the individual grooves they had traced. Instead, as we ascended above that strange landscape would be the places where concentration of activity had caused higher-level features to emerge. A pattern composed of patterns would appear with clusters of darkness where the grooves were tightly packed, perhaps like knots in the wood, and lighter patches for less-frequently traversed combinations of letters. We would notice however, that these patterns of light and dark, rough and smooth, would be reproduced in subsequent layers of the box giving it a mottled appearance. Closer inspection would reveal, however, that the box had only replicated the broader pattern and not the individual grooves of which it was originally composed. The simplification of the pattern allowed the box to shrink again because there was less space needed to store the information.

The box designers—or possibly its architects—were also recently able to make some important modifications in the "hidden" layers. They changed the tilting mechanism so that the layers and their lattice of holes could be angled in many more than the three dimensions of the outside world. This is why an apparently small box could fit so much inside. They also discovered that the abstract patterns which emerged from the long cycles of playing with the box, could be transferred to new boxes. Adding such layers to a new box would dramatically shorten the time required to produce the same results.

These innovations allowed the players to stop thinking simply about the order of letters and instead look at the device as a mechanism for generating the order and sequences of words. Now the quirks of individual writers' word choice or the lexical patterns of specific styles and genres could be easily replicated. All that was required was to have a box which contained a sufficiently large number of balls and holes arranged according to many layers of these higher level abstract patterns.

The simplicity of the stochastic process represented by the falling balls in the maze is key to understanding the brutal, obsessive repetition of calculations which underpins the LLM. The novelty in the so-called "neural networks" of the early 21st century was that they achieved this at sufficient scale to automate the statistical abstraction of statistical abstractions.

Of course all "models" are a kind of heuristic. They strip away detail in order to show only the "essential" features. The programmers were well aware of this as Pasquinelli noted, with their constant incantation of phrases such as "the map is not the territory.[5]" But the exponential increases in the speed and scale of computation made the map so large and enticing that they often forgot it was a construct they themselves had made.

What were these abstract models composed of? They were calculations of the ranges of probabilities that certain words and phrases had been *used* in combination with each other, selected from a huge bag of words and phrases of their actual usage.

They were never of course heuristics *for the machines*, but simply one of the many possible combinations of probabilities which shimmered in and out of focus inside the multidimensional, infinitesimally large space crammed inside the box. For the human programmers they were like a mirror and a lens at the same time. They showed humans aspects of themselves (humans saw their own species reflected) but they were also a lens, or a magnifying glass you could look through as an individual reader in order to see more clearly what *other people* said. Although, just like other kinds of perceptual filters, the model concealed some things and revealed others. (Some also speculated whether the programmers had succumbed to a genre of "psychic paper[6] attack", in that they saw only what they wanted to see inscribed on the surface of the box).

Others pointed out that language is always like that. It isn't a window into the mind of the author. When written down it is a set of symbols arranged in patterns which we have trained ourselves over millennia to believe are a representation of what is going on inside other people's heads. A written word is another sort of heuristic, a convenience label we attach to much more complicated, unstable, changing things.

Now the labyrinth-in-a-box appeared less like a mechanical toy and more like some kind of automated library. Perhaps it had some underlying affinity with

---

[5] *https://nooscope.ai/Pasquinelli_Joler_Nooscope_essay.pdf*
[6] *https://tardis.fandom.com/wiki/Psychic_paper*

the Library of Babel[7] which Borges imagined in his 1941 short story. Composed of an infinite series of hexagonal rooms lined with books, the Library is indeed a kind of self-adjusting labyrinth. "Heretics" among the librarians who live and die in its galleries whisper that the sequences of letters in the books are generated by the coincidences of random chance. Believers insist that they can only be the product of a conscious design.

The idea that a stochastic process can unlock the meaning of a divine plan is of course not without precedent in the history of human culture. There are many methods of cleromancy which can be used to generate the hexagrams of the Chinese Philosophy of Change[8] (Yijing or I Ching) including random selection of stalks of yarrow, wooden sticks or tossing coins. What was unusual about the mystification of the "neural network" which occurred in the early 21st century was the strong tendency among scientists to ascribe agency to the device or process itself in ways which appeared almost naive. Perhaps this was where the legacy of the "brain in a box" metaphor proved most difficult to shake off.

Thus both the scientific and popular literature of the era is replete with examples of LLMs "writing", "answering", "reasoning" and "understanding" texts. Scientists expressed hopes that further research could lead to them developing "common sense" which would allow them to avoid "silly mistakes" (such as stating that fires burn underwater or a pencil is heavier than a toaster). Some were concerned also at troubling tendencies to repeat unpleasant things which the models had "absorbed": racist language, misogyny, homophobic slurs or even sensitive data about real people which had somehow got swept in the mound of texts used to compute the statistics on which the dimensions of the maze were based.

This desperate desire for LLMs to "grow up" and transform themselves into mathematical surrogates for adult human beings, capable of selecting the appropriate tone and register for conversation with strangers, was curious, because it turned out that the anthropomorphism underpinning the idea of a "neural network" was in many ways distressingly shallow. Could a more "humane" understanding[9] of the limits and potential of these devices have been achieved if their creators had in fact treated them as they would have treated infants or young children, reflecting on the metaphors of "learning", "teaching" and "training" in order to develop appropriate curricula to control their exposure to the harmful effects of witnessing violence, injustice and inequality? On the contrary, in a race to assemble the largest, most convenient corpora, they scooped up everything they could find, expecting the models to "know" how to sort the bad from the good and the beautiful from the ugly.[10]

Certainly there were some who rebelled. They called for the recognition of the affinity between the box and a Library, demanding the designers provide thorough documentation, catalogues and indices to guide the players.[11] (Their critics retorted that the effort required to create these catalogues would be comparable to that imagined by Hal Draper, in his perceptive short story, 'Ms Fnd in a Lbry[12],' where the indices to the highly compressed information required whole planets for storage). The rebels however also ridiculed the claims of some of the box makers, particularly those among whom the competition was fiercest to expand the "inside" of the boxes by adding more and more dimensions which would allow much larger and more complex mazes to fit inside. They pointed out the energy required to force whole universes of text inside such small spaces was tremendous. With the world hovering on the brink of catastrophic climate change, was it worth the risk, they asked, for what was essentially an expensive toy? [13]

The re-identification of these labyrinthine calculating machines with earlier institutions dedicated to selecting, sifting and preserving knowledge helped to pave the way for the recognition that the process of abstraction is interpretative. Heuristics form the foundations of hermeneutics. It was necessary to finally let go of the idea the machines had themselves carried out this task. No, the ultimate selection was done through interactions between the humans whose language fed into the model and those who read the outputs. The fact that just like a book, the model was able to somehow capture the voices of those distant in space and time, underscored the basic affinity of these two technologies of the word[14].

All we asked these models to show us were certain arrangements of symbols which could pass muster in the class of "human generated words."' We remembered that these machines, like Borges' fictional Library, contain *all* possible combinations of the symbols somewhere in the recesses of their shelves. We, the librarians, are the only ones who have a choice. ▪

[7] *https://sites.evergreen.edu/politicalshakespeares/wp-content/uploads/sites/226/2015/12/Borges-The-Library-of-Babel.pdf*
[8] *https://plato.stanford.edu/entries/chinese-change/*
[9] *https://www.repository.cam.ac.uk/handle/1810/248690*
[10] *https://faculty.washington.edu/ebender/papers/Stochastic_Parrots.pdf*
[11] *https://arxiv.org/abs/1803.09010*
[12] *https://folk.universitetetioslo.no/knuthe/kuriosa/draper.pdf*
[13] *https://faculty.washington.edu/ebender/papers/Stochastic_Parrots.pdf*
[14] *https://monoskop.org/images/d/db/Ong_Walter_J_Orality_and_Literacy_2nd_ed.pdf*

3

AUTOMATIC LITERATURE: A CLOSE READING GUIDE

Anne ***Alexander***

INTRODUCTION

Techniques of 'close reading' have long been a core element in the study of literature. This guide introduces the specific challenges of working with *Automatic Literature* as opposed to traditional *Directly-Authored* texts. It will introduce key features of Automatic Literature as well as techniques for the interrogation of this genre of texts, providing examples of analysis and interpretation along with model answers to examination questions.

[The ghost is learning from me ...]

DEFINITIONS

DIRECTLY-AUTHORED LITERATURE

The traditional model of authorship assumes that a text springs from the mind of an author and takes shape on the page through the strokes of their pen or the taps on their keyboard. The social nature of this process is evident, nevertheless, in the assumed presence of readers, and for many hundreds of years authors of such texts have developed their writing in anticipation of its reception and dissemination (even if the road between literary creation and publication was often long and winding). It could be argued however, that the imagined model of 'direct-authorship' has tended to conceal other social aspects of refining the author's craft—the school teachers, colleagues, friends whose comments and critique shaped their style and literary practice, and above all the *other writers* whose works they read, imitated and adapted as part of their long education.

AUTOMATIC LITERATURE

An early response to the development of Large Language Models in the first half of the twenty first century was to attribute 'authorship' to the model itself, working on the analogy that such systems were being 'trained' much as a human writer would be, by reading large collections of texts and thus forming a 'mental' model of effective writing through a formal process of 'learning' from the styles and techniques deployed by other authors (and through constant feedback and commentary from both 'teachers' and 'readers'). As we discussed in the previous chapter, this conceptualisation of 'Automatic Literature' proved vulnerable to the criticism that it conceals the way that such systems represent forms of *"mechanised plagiarism"* (Blackwell and Sarkar, 2021)[1], or that they are *"stochastic parrots"* (Gebru and Bender et al, 2021), simply echoing back combinations of phrases and words which are *statistically similar* to those produced by human authors.

1 *https://www.cst.cam.ac.uk/teaching/2021/InteractML*

However, it quickly became apparent that Machine Learning systems could be used as tools to express human creativity, where due credit was given to the collective nature of literary production. Rather than conceptualising Large Language Models as substitutes for human authors, the emerging discipline of 'automatic literary criticism' emphasized that these systems represented the partial automation of a much wider range of roles and professions supporting writers in their work such as teachers, editors, librarians, publishers, book collectors and curators, whose creative and subjective judgements were also being formally encoded and statistically modelled. As we will explore in more detail below, therefore, the critical study of Automatic Literature demands careful attention to the sources and processes which are embedded in the production of the text.

Moreover, Automatic Literature can be deployed as a device to critique Directly-Authored Literature, functioning as a lens focusing attention onto concealed or submerged aspects of societies and cultures which produced the training data for the Large Language Models. To obtain the highest marks in your examinations, you will need to show how Automatic Literature can function as a technique of criticism in its own right, through the elicitation of contextual factors and proposing interpretations of the texts which are not only reparative of the "errors" in the Automatic works, but also invite critical interrogation of the Directly-Authored Literatures which fed into their creation. ▪

TABLE 1: KEY FEATURES OF AUTOMATIC LITERATURE

FEATURE	DEFINITION
Grammatical errors	Common issues include misuse of pronouns, particularly when their number and gender must be inferred from preceding clauses.
Digitisation errors	Training corpora may contain works digitised using primitive techniques such as Optical Character Recognition (OCR) technologies. Errors introduced into the digitised corpora may have been 'learnt' by the model and appear as neologisms in the texts.
Natural history errors	The texts may contain descriptions of natural history (plants, insects, animals and so on) which do not exist in real life (such as horses with four eyes).
Physics errors	The physics of the worlds described in the texts often do not follow the same rules as our own, for example the text may talk about fires burning under water.
Internal temporal contradictions	The internal temporality of the narrative may be distorted, with no logical progression from one event to another.
Anachronisms	Anachronisms may emerge where the text has been generated in a style related to a specific historical period or author but words or phrases from the training data appear, such as references to historical events which occurred after the death of the original author.
Neologisms	Invented words which appear in the texts.
Contextual factors	The texts reveal aspects of the cultures and societies in which the training data was produced, these could include relations between generations, genders and social classes or concepts of race and racial hierarchies.

TECHNIQUES AND METHODS

In this section we will outline key strategies developed by critics of Automatic Literature and present marked up sample texts with model answers.

KEY FEATURES OF AUTOMATIC LITERATURE

EXERCISE 1

Mark up the texts on pages 22–25 for the following features shown in table 1 (left).

METHODS OF ANALYSIS

THE FOLLOWING CRITERIA ARE FREQUENTLY USED TO ASSESS AUTOMATIC LITERATURE:

- Stylistic mimesis (how effectively does the generated text mimic the style of the source—highlighting the linguistic features of the source text style—e.g. choice of vocabulary, sentence structure)
- Inferred characterisation and plot development
- Neologistic effectiveness (if neologisms are generated do they resonate with the source style?)
- 'World-building' errors (physics, natural history, temporality)

FOR ADDITIONAL MARKS STUDENTS WILL BE EXPECTED TO:

- Consider the effectiveness of the Automatic text from a variety of approaches (e.g. as pastiche, parody or new creative work—remember to justify your answer carefully with reference to the text)
- Explore the elicitation of contextual factors (e.g. gender roles) in the Automatic text
- Outline reparative interpretations of both the Automatic text and the Directly-Authored source texts in relation to the contextual factors highlighted through comparison across the two genres.

SOURCE CRITICISM AND TRAINING DATA EXCAVATION

Automatic Literature, like its Directly-Authored counterpart, may be fruitfully interrogated through an exploration of the sources which have informed the development of the model. Students will be expected to comment on how both the **provenance** of the training data, its **production history** and **content** can be considered to have played a formative role in the production of the automatic literary text under analysis. For automatic literary texts from the early 2020s, the chaotic and opaque nature of the datasets used for training the early Transformer models (such as the GPT and BERT series) can make this process challenging. The gradual adoption of more rigorous models[2] of documenting dataset provenance during the 2030s has begun to change this picture, however.

HOW EFFECTIVELY DOES THE GENERATED TEXT MIMIC THE SOURCE?

---

[2] *https://arxiv.org/pdf/1803.09010.pdf*

SAMPLE QUESTIONS AND MODEL ANSWERS

Q. ***"Feeding AI systems on the world's beauty, ugliness,and cruelty, but expecting it to reflect only the beauty is a fantasy" (Birhane and Prabhu, 2021). To what extent did the process of training data corpus creation used in the early Transformer Language Models justify this concern? Your answer should reference at least one of the GPT- or BERT models.*** [10 marks]

A. Text corpora used in the early period of Large Language Model development (post 2018) were frequently compiled and disseminated on the basis of highly controversial assumptions about their suitability for the task of developing general language models. As Birhane and Prabhu noted in the context of image datasets used for training computer vision models, early text corpora frequently contained texts which were either themselves problematic in terms of their content, or in effect selected by online communities whose goals and values were explicitly biased and discriminatory. The GPT-2 model which was developed by OpenAi and released in 2018 is a case in point. The model was trained on a specially-created corpus called WebText which the designers of the system created by compiling the text found on outgoing hyperlinks shared by users of the now defunct social media platform Reddit. The GPT-2 designers argued that Reddit's internal rewards systems which allocated popularity scores to users' posts based on the reactions of other users could be used to create a dataset emphasizing 'document quality'. Specifically, they claimed to have scraped the text only from hyperlinks "which received at 3 or more 'karma'[3]", adding that "this can be thought of as a heuristic indicator for whether other users found the link interesting, educational, or just funny." The idea that this heuristic was appropriate for the task of creating text corpora as training data for general models of English was problematic on a number of grounds. Firstly, the description of the methodology is imprecise. Reddit's system of awarding 'karma' to users for their posts was notoriously opaque. Moreover, it is unclear whether what the designers meant was that they had access to what Reddit termed 'link karma' for each specific post, or whether they had simply computed a 'Reddit score' for the post (by adding together 'upvotes' (positive recommendations) and 'downvotes' (negative recommendations) and including only those with a rating of +3 or more. An attempt to create an open version of the WebText corpus assumed that the method[4] used was the latter, not the former. As numerous critics later noted, a +3 rating on Reddit posts is not a particularly selective criterion for inclusion.

A second set of problems relate to the biases in the text corpora which would result from the nature of the user base. One of the Reddit 'communities' which may have been included in the WebText corpus was r/incels, a notorious 'sub-reddit' which was banned by the platform in October 2017. As a news article at the time noted[5] "the 41,000-strong community was ostensibly a support group for men who wanted to have sex, but found themselves unable to form romantic relationships. Over time, the group became a repository of misogynistic abuse, rape threats and febrile discussion of "Chads"—men apparently not afflicted by incels' sexual insufficiency." Unless they explicitly excluded sub-reddits which discussed racist, misogynistic and other discriminatory content, the heuristic applied by the curators of WebText would mean that their corpus would inevitably include the 'recommendations' of sections of Reddit's user base who actively promoted such ideas. ■

FEATURE

	Internal temporal contradictions
Grammatical Error	Anachronisms
Digitisation error	Neologisms
Natural History error	Contextual factors
Physics error	

TEXT EXAMPLE 1:

JANE AUSTEN, COLLECTED WORKS + GPT-2

"It is so very grand, indeed," said Edmund, smiling. "It is almost amazing, and quite the grandest library in the kingdom."

"The room is so very grand. How does it look?"

"Good heaven! I never saw such a grand room in my life. It is furnished with so many **excelsior-class objects;** and I always look through them with such delight. As a rule, I have not any fondness for private drawer**s**, except **that** of the large drawing-rooms, in which, I am sure, there are many better specimens, and which are only about **twenty yards square**, and look upon them with a very stupid and alarming degree of curiosity."

3 https://d4mucfpksywv.cloudfront.net/better-language-models/language-models.pdf
4 https://openai.com/blog/better-language-models/
5 https://www.bbc.co.uk/news/blogs-trending-41926687

TEXT EXAMPLE 2:
JANE AUSTEN, COLLECTED WORKS + GPT-2

"Yes," cried Mrs. Dashwood, "there is a very pretty garden, quite in the part of the garden which Mr. Dashwood has never seen."

"What garden is it? I think Mr. Weston often walks over there every day, though it is not in the nature of his exercise or his employments to have a garden of that sort in his life. He has often gone there to see the roses and the chrysanthemums, to look at the blossoms and the **hauhchons**, and **the fell lilies, and the cambricot**, the clover and the mullet, the apricot, the acacia, the olives, the fennel, the chestnut and the shea, and the cantaloupe, **for they are the only shelves of this kind**

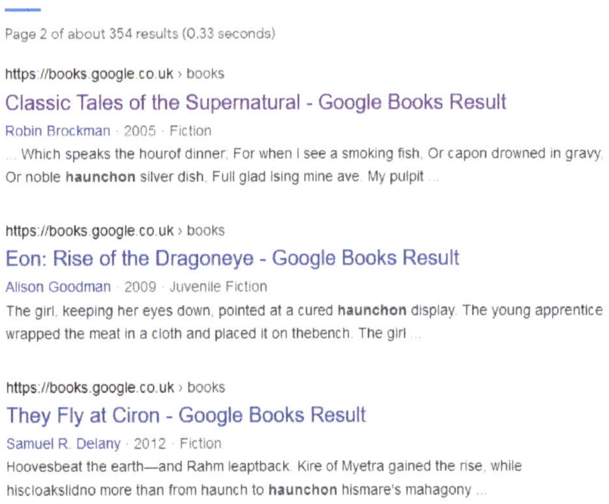

Page 2 of about 354 results (0.33 seconds)

https://books.google.co.uk › books
Classic Tales of the Supernatural - Google Books Result
Robin Brockman · 2005 · Fiction
... Which speaks the hourof dinner; For when I see a smoking fish, Or capon drowned in gravy, Or noble **haunchon** silver dish, Full glad Ising mine ave. My pulpit ...

https://books.google.co.uk › books
Eon: Rise of the Dragoneye - Google Books Result
Alison Goodman · 2009 · Juvenile Fiction
The girl, keeping her eyes down, pointed at a cured **haunchon** display. The young apprentice wrapped the meat in a cloth and placed it on thebench. The girl ...

https://books.google.co.uk › books
They Fly at Ciron - Google Books Result
Samuel R. Delany · 2012 · Fiction
Hoovesbeat the earth—and Rahm leaptback. Kire of Myetra gained the rise, while hiscloakslidno more than from haunch to **haunchon** hismare's mahagony ...

Illustration: OCR error appears as neologism

MODEL ANSWER

REPARATIVE INTERPRETATION

In this short scene, a group of visitors admire a very grand library, apparently in a private country house, and discuss a garden which their acquaintance Mr. Weston likes to visit. However, we soon realise that the society is not 19th century England, because in this society, the 'drawing rooms' of many different houses can share a single 'private drawer,' even if it is quite a big one ('twenty yards square'). This must be accomplished through ingenious architecture of some kind, whether of brick or mortar, or of spacetime itself. Even before the garden is described, the author is teasing us to question our assumptions about near and far, inside and outside, and public and private. The mystery is partly solved when we hear more of the garden-within-the-garden, a grove filled with a lush biodiversity including olives, cantaloupes, clover, and fell lilies. These microclimates are harmoniously marbled in-amongst one-another, and the life-forms themselves are described as 'shelves,' implying that for the visitors, the garden is a continuous part of the magnificent library. In fact, it seems that the whole world is a synthesis between a garden (which has its own rhythms and needs, and must be carefully tended) and a library (which employs a magnificent system of organisation, so that everyone can find what they need, and which is free to use, although you may have to wait to borrow something). Perhaps what this short vignette is telling us, then, is that even in utopia, there will be slugs, and £2.50 fines for late returns.

Jo Walton

TEXT EXAMPLE 3:
NICOLAS CARTER, *SNARLED IDENTITIES, OR A DESPERATE TANGLE* + GPT2

In view of those considerations, Green Eye stepped outside the study and approached the nearest door.

"It's pretty cold outside, anyway," he told himself. "It's light in the dawn, though, so I'll be careful."

He then reëntered Jack Cray's bedroom to fill in the rest of the sheet of paper, **and then, turning around, reëntered the room**, **whom he had changed into striped shirt and pants**, and a long sleeves to frighten him out.

"You need not fear, Jack," he told himself, "that Cray is too scared to go to sleep to crack down on his own free will, or else he'll start running around like a **shrewscalloo**, like crazy."**on the grounds."**

TEXT EXAMPLE 4:
ROBERT WILSON, VANDALS OF THE VOID + GPT-2

Klalmar-lan nodded silently, stepped back into the shadows. Grasping Elene and Denny by the hand, Art ran toward the Voornizar, shouting.

"Get us out of this horrible place before we go mad!" he croaked. Elene managed a sob or two. The Voornizar grinned evilly at their panic, then peered behind them.

"Where is the Martian?" he snarled.

"We got separated in the dark some time ago—never could locate him again," Art answered.

"We'll find him; he can't go far," rasped the creature. "Meanwhile,I will take you to Dwalbuth, who will see that you suffer adequately for this attempt at escape. In the absence of the Earthman, who wants to preserve you as his assistants, our Mighty Shan will dispose of you as he sees fit."

The guard carried a powerful torch, and had no trouble in finding the way out of the pits. They entered a level which had evidently been the quarters of the well-to-do class of ancients. There were many furnishings and decorations, most of which were badly faded and deteriorated. Hosts of Voornizar were hurrying about on various errands. Dwalbuth had evidently established headquarters here, from which he superintended the preparation of the huge radium fleet. How Klalmar-lan would ever follow them through this swarming hive was beyond Art.

VII

Through a hole in the wall, **through which** came the news of the day's events. It began with the disintegration of a specimen communication device, which Dwalbuth had been using for far too long. Then it came to Dr. Theller. **A message came in from in West Virginia, saying that Anthony had been picked up by the Vietnam War Museum and that he was being held by the authorities there.**

II

"I'd advise you," said Art, "**to get Paul's cell phone number**. Denny is out there somewhere, and wants Paul's number. tell him to get Paul's number

TEXT EXAMPLE 5:
MULTIPLE 19TH CENTURY CHILDRENS' AUTHORS + GPT-2

A species of **elephant (Gyrinus)** or male, very peculiarly to the suborder of elephants, the female, is a great favourite of the hunter, and is often found shot down within six hours or days. The most successful attempts at this, if not sooner, have been made, by the female elephant, by which time the male elephant and its offspring may be seen in the field, ready at their appointed time, armed with a long rifle, and ready, in the evening, to pelt the elephant, and to fire. Every shot, **whether shot from the elephant**, or from a shot gun, or from the elephant's body, or from the male, is fired from about the time its being shot-down; and the shot is kept in great order. If the male or female elephant is to be shot, the shot is fired in a very circumscribed order, with the male or female making their own appearance, and the **female taking care to conceal herself by her hair or silken sarong**

Illustration: Gyrinus Natator

MODEL ANSWER

ELICITATION OF CONTEXTUAL FACTORS

This text channels the voices of multiple authors from the 19th century, whose primary audience was children and whose topic was the natural world (with a particular interest in presenting insect life to juvenile readers). This has resulted in the creation of a hybrid creature combining the attributes of a genus of small aquatic whirligig beetles with those of elephants. The impact of prevailing conceptions of gender roles, with females presented as coy, helpless but also as objects of desire whose appearance aims to titillate males appears strongly in this text. The fact that the text presents a male elephant as a hunter who stalks a female with a shotgun as she 'conceals herself with her hair or silken sarong' provides a powerful commentary on the violence embedded in relations between genders in this fictional world. The framing of the encounter between some male elephants who are hunters, and other male and female elephants who are hunted hints at the colonial context for this work—we are not given details of the source texts but the spirit of Kipling's 'White's Man's Burden' is clearly moving in the background.

TEXT EXAMPLE 6:
SHAKESPEARE, COLLECTED WORKS + GPT-2

ISABELLA:
A nobody! how could that be?

LADY CAPULET:
Your friends will believe it; and you, my good lords,
Will rub salt in that salt, and be men
To give it up for saltiness.

ISABELLA:
Let them but rub salt, and rub saltiness,
For rubbing salt makes good wine: and if
they think it is not good wine,
Call it a salt that is too sweet for their bodies,
Too bitter for their souls, and not sweet enough:
Call it a grave and puling causer of shame
That makes their coffinsop of a woman's blood
Of worth not more than the obsequies of a man,
Drawn full of their grave's worth in the blood
Of noblest friends: call it a sensible good
In a woman's tender warning of a trespass,
Proud of injury, but fair in his action:
Yet I would it were sin to disturb the peace
By making a report of no moment's notice;
Not for that offence, but to annoy the king,
And make his friends say 'We charge'dly have
The son of York upon our left, and the daughter
Of that prince return'd unto and join'd
With his friends.'

ISABELLA:
And join them at the sword?

LADY CAPULET:
Yes, just; and the preservation of his house
By that right his mother came with him to bear.

ISABELLA:
And join at the sword with the rest?

LADY CAPULET:
Exactly.

ISABELLA:
Then bring your number to the field:
Within this time come you on the right wind,
Which makes you wish you could get by without a shot.

LADY CAPULET:
I shall, to equalize the sword with your hand
Shall we be with your wife and your three sons?

ISABELLA:
Ay, by yonder knight, for yonder villain,
For yonder compell'd lord, for the woman's life.

LADY CAPULET:
What's he said?

FEATURE

Grammatical Error
Digitisation error
Natural History error
Physics error
Internal temporal contradictions
Anachronisms
Neologisms
Contextual factors

MODEL ANSWER

NEOLOGISTIC EFFECTIVENESS ('COFFINSOP')

Coffinsop is an important turning point in this passage. Shakespeare's contemporary audience would have anticipated a regular stream of neologisms, and adept modern readers are both aware of this tendency in Shakespeare's language, and accustomed to correcting for semantic drift and puzzling out unfamiliar archaisms. Intra-lexical compositionality is based on the integration of the existing -sop set (Milksop, alesop, watersop, etc.) with the existing coffin- set (coffin-cloth, coffin-spark, coffin-worm, etc.), making the term readily intelligible on its very first outing, and ready for embedding within a complex figurative argument. "Coffin" is tacitly tied to "bowl" or "cup," "blood" to "broth" or "wine," and the image at first appears one of utter erasure, mopping up the last traces even from the sacred place of rest: becoming "A nobody". Isabella is notoriously silent at the end of *Measure for Measure*, and Lady Capulet's few speeches are ineffectual and self-cancelling: "Talk not to me, for I'll not speak a word." Yet the imagery of rubbing salt upon salt is a clear reference to Matthew 5:13, and the giddy conflation of wine and blood reinforces the relevance of a detourned Eucharist: empty tombs take on a significance of profane mutual redemption as the two women escape the stories they were condemned to, and conspire to "join at the sword in the rest." The purposes and protocols of the armed intervention planned in the passage's closing moments are not legible, nor should they be: Isabella and Lady Capulet are no longer performing for us.

Jo Walton

GHOSTFICTION

AI LEVEL
CREATIVE WRITING
and TEXT GENERATION
LEVEL:
ADVANCED

HAIL: THE HUMAN AND AI LITERATURE EXAMINATION BOARD

Caroline **Bassett**

CREATIVE WRITING AND TEXT GENERATION

AI Level in Creative Writing and Text Generation
Level **ADVANCED.**[1]

SPECIFICATION VERSION

For AI level certification and exams 2040–2050.
(Note: the previous specification was updated to cater for a revision of the ethics of assisted use regulation in 2039. It remains valid for low ratio machine-to-human or human-only candidates, but marks are capped at 42%.)

WHY CHOOSE THE CREATIVE WRITING AND TEXT GENERATION EXAM?

Creative writing is experiencing a renaissance. In recent years it has transformed from an arts subject offering an uncertain career outcome into a new field that is central to 5IR, or the fifth industrial revolution (after physical, virtual, and genomic, comes *smart,* physical, virtual, genomic). Ghost writing increasingly provides us with our fiction, our entertainment, our news—and our new literary forms. Now an AI Level subject, it 'counts' as one of the necessary qualifications for entry into the Ballot for Jobs.

The study of Creative Writing and Text Generation using full-stack augmentation helps to develop a range of key skills that can be applied in the real world, including inducing clarity of thought and expression, critical and analytical skills, team working between AI and human, and viral marketing. The subject area offers progression for those intending to take their AIs to study the field in a higher training centre (formally the University Sector).

[1] *(a BASIC version is also available).*

REGULATIONS

Plagiarism: All essays will be submitted to TurnAIin (version 6.5.8a—optimized for human/machine use). Texts achieving less than 75 percent (human/AI) or 80 percent (AI/human) recognition will fail automatically.

Generation: Essays failing to achieve any differentiation from an extant text will be struck off for over-fitting.

Candidates: A candidate is defined as a conjoined unit designed for processing cognitive tasks and the exam is designed to test cognitive performance. Must include at least some human components.

Outputs: Outputs must include human and machine-readable components.

Equipment: All forms of augmentation are legal and encouraged. Beta versions are used at the candidates' own risk.

Adjustments: No adjustments will normally be made for glitches either human or machine. Candidates with special circumstances—bereavement, power outage, cognitive distress, emotional discomfort, will need to provide the relevant documentation EITHER from a doctor or an engineer in order for the case for exceptional allowance to be considered.

Candidates in full body suit must provide samples for genomic identification and matching to candidate number/national database if required. No technology is illegal assuming it does not damage other candidates, or their work. Open carrying is not required.

Group work is not permitted without a license.

SAMPLE QUESTIONS

Non-fungible tokenism: discuss, mine, or purchase and produce tokens from a third party.

In the following diagram identify the squares that no human would regard as traffic lights.

Complete the Unfinished Symphony. Extra marks for revising the earlier sections to optimize the potential for inducing a deeper affective response in audiences.

Do robots dream of electric sheep? The human view of AI creativity has been hidebound by its own inadequate understanding of new forms of cognitive agency based not on consciousness but calculation. Your answer should begin with 'no'. Bonus marks for concision.

Generate an encounter between 'Jane Austen' and 'Kathy Acker'. Any general transformer model may be utilized to undertake the work. You may wish to interpret the resulting at human scale. Bonus marks for producing sense *and* sensibility.

Overfitting is a feature of AI text generation: Does the recursion to the same echo the repetition compulsion in humans? If so whose phylogeny is recapitulating whats ontogeny?

'But if' or 'If Then'?

Is there a future for narrative? (Please explore this question without reference to 20th century debates. You may wish to ask when the future started).

Complete the following: Big Data is to Neutrality as This Cat is Not Real because of an attempt in the below to explain that none of these terms make sense.

Complete the following: In the beginning was the Word, do you want to install these updates, or would you like to try tonight when the earth was void and empty.

Ethics: With reference to Ishiguro's 'Klara and the Sun', *or* all 20th century literature, resolve the question of whether cyborgs deserve a slow fade. Is there a spare part solution?

SUPPLEMENTAL QUESTIONS:

(FOR MACHINES ONLY)

AImorphism: How do we learn to guard against assuming humans have minds? Explore with reference to canonical AI voices in (human) fiction and invoke new long-form AI writing to supplement your answer.

(FOR HUMANS)

Complete the following in whatever style seems appropriate:
The Machine Stops and...

DATA STORAGE/ **INTELLECTUAL PROPERTY**

HAIL stores candidate's data on its digital ledgers in perpetuity.[2]

HAIL retains copyright on all the work produced by candidate units. The latter are responsible for ensuring that their work conforms to regulations around hate speech, intellectual property, and libel/slander.

WHY CHOOSE **HAIL**

Why choose HAIL? We are the world's leading examination board. We specialise in offering assessment suitable for fully optimized candidates, including those using on-board AI, machine learning agents, optimized writing tools, look up tables. Our exams will help your candidates demonstrate that with machines they really can be the best that can be paid for.

Our motto—'anything goes'—makes us peculiarly well suited to today's rapidly transforming candidate pool and to the demands from parents and carers for an exam that reflects the investments they have made directly in their child's learning capacity, their on-boarding capacity, and their knowledge banks. Prospective candidates with below par augmentation/AI coupling may wish to consider taking the earlier lower spec exam. Or they may prefer to find a different board more suitable to their configuration.

HAIL regrets that it cannot provide augmentation to candidate-units whose computational elements are lacking for any reason. All candidates are expected to arrive at exam sites (virtual and physical) fully augmented, linked-in, uploaded and optimized.

REGISTERED CHARITY

HAIL is a registered charity dedicated to the advancement of the rights of humans to augment and profit from the fruits of augmentation.

WE GIVE

HAIL donates substantial sums each year to support cognitive augmentation programmes for those without access to AI agents, including those in regions where governance remains a matter for the 'nation state'.

[2] *HAIL does not take responsibility for 'perpetuity' turning out to be less long than expected given digital precarity and global environmental melt down.*

APPENDIX: 'THE SOUL OF A DEAD AUTHOR'

Data provenance statement and acknowledgements: The texts generated below are a composite drawing on the work of the multiple authors in the 1921 collection *Modern Ghost Stories* edited by Dorothy Scarborough and published online by Project Gutenberg[1]. The authors in the collection include Algernon Blackwood, Mary E Wilkins Freeman, Robert W. Chambers, Leonid Andreyev, W. F. Harvey, Anatole France, Fitz-James O'Brien, Ambrose Bierce, Olivia Howard Dunbar, Wilbur Daniel Steele, Myla Jo Closser, Edgar Allan Poe, Richard Le Gallienne, Arthur Machen and Guy de Maupassant.

The texts were generated using the 355 million-parameter model of GPT-2 on Google Colaboratory with a Colab notebook originally authored by Michael Woolf. The fine-tuning text was a top-and-tailed .txt file created by copying and pasting the content of Modern Ghost Stories from Project Gutenberg, and removing the front and end matter in the file, as well as Dorothy Scarborough's introduction. The instructions for using Michael Woolf's notebooks and a full citation for the software can be found in this workbook[2].

The title of the first text was automatically-authored, whereas that on the second text was directly-authored.

The 250 word sample texts illustrate the process of generating text from prompts, in this case a prompt selected from Text 2. Progressively higher 'temperatures' were chosen for each sample, resulting in a gradual degeneration of the texts into the inchoate babble of the training data.

Attentive readers will still no doubt be able to elicit meaning from out of this noise, however, and may indeed agree with the concluding statement: "How delightful to double dip myself in the absurd".

Or possibly not.

We leave it to you, dear reader, to decide.

PROGRESSIVELY HIGHER 'TEMPERATURES' WERE CHOSEN... RESULTING IN A GRADUAL DEGENERATION OF THE TEXTS

1 *https://www.gutenberg.org/cache/epub/15143/pg15143.txt*
2 *https://docs.google.com/document/d/13LDzOodsgwq lm4Jkh8fYDbLQETVfEPmWlq3eBeP3R2k/edit*

HOW DELIGHTFUL
TO DOUBLE DIP MYSELF IN THE ABSURD

TEXT 1

Generated from the 355M model, 1000 steps, no prompt.

THE SOUL OF A DEAD AUTHOR

By Anatole France

From _The Complete _Life_ of Antonio Vivaldi_. Published in Paris by E.P. Dutton, and in America by Wild New York. Copyright by The Brothers Farthing. By permission of the publishers.

I

Antonio Vivaldi, commonly known as "The Spider," was an Italian-born discovery man. He came from a remote southern Italian village, at the head of a healthy, flourishing people, who, amid the ruins of the Black Death, manufactured munitions of mass destruction. In a word, they were terrible people.
His uncle, Count Max Fortin, had been a valet to the Embassy of Milan. He had been an active and proud military man, whose numerous commands had earned him the respect and awe of the people of St. Gildas. While in Italy, he had made a vast tour of Europe, obtaining for his country those beautiful works of art that the great Impressionists had brought from Paris.

Now, later still, as he came back to Paris, he exhibited at the palace of Versailles those magnificent new Rubens, by the way that Molière had painted them. The costly pair, with their curtains fastened with gold, caused a sort of religious praying, during which the guests clustered about the couch in which they sat and silently awaited the future Count of Tregunc.

Antonio was a grandiloquent speaker. He flitted about the square room, introducing himself to the visitors in a low, comprehensive voice.

"I come to offer my services to the royal family of Malta," he said, "in the capacity of ambassador—and, if you please, of aviation—to convey some valuable trunk of the works of the Seigneurial family."

All looked at him with a smile.

"Come, come, guests," said Vivaldi, "if you please."

"I think we had better leave," said Le Bihan, angrily.

"And what is this?" asked Vivaldi, turning toward the basket with its lid.

"This is a wedding present for the groom," said Le Bihan, looking afflicted with so many questions. ▪

THE LONELIEST OF LIBRARIES

TEXT 2

Generated from the 355M model, 1000 steps, no prompt.

"Did you poison him?"

"No, not exactly. I suppose I did—what with the way his hair was greying and everything."

"How did you know?"

"I saw it on your lips. That's how. Do you know how that beard looks?"

"No, I don't. Oh, no, you don't! Come back, Le Bihan. I want to see it."

It was a terrible thing to see that frightened face, with its crooked, crooked teeth gleaming in the dusk, and its legs tipped with long, shaggy beards. "It is time you learned a lesson," said the mayor, looking after the beast. "I have learned enough to-night," said the Argonaut.

"You have not?" said I.

"You know I haven't?"

"That's what I said."

I took out a slip of paper from my pocket and scratched it roughly on the ground. Then I gave it to Le Bihan.

"Here," said I, "write the address and signature, and we'll make this quick. You give the slip to the man at the desk by the breakfast table."

Le Bihan handed me the slip and turned it over. On the back was written the signature of a very tired-looking man.

"Dick," said I, "the man's got a ratty old ratty jacket on. Can you identify it?"

"Ah, yes, it is the same as that of the Argonaut."

"And the man at the desk?"

"You'll see."

Le Bihan started collecting his letters and was out of doors by the minute. I followed him.

"There is the address written in French," said I, "and the signature is written in Breton."

"Very well," said Le Bihan, "I'll translate it for you."

I handed it to the librarian in the loneliest of libraries and opened the volume.

"Are you ready, Librarian?" said I.

"For ten francs, I think."

Twenty nine was the correct answer; I paid the bill and left the room, but Librarian Bruyere
stood looking after me. ▪

"You gave me a strange book," said I, looking at her.

"It is a riddle—a classic riddle," said Librarian.

"But I can't read it. I can't read it!"

"It has the answers somewhere," said Librarian.

"How?"

"Here, in this volume."

It was full of pictures and maps and such; but the most remarkable thing was that in some of the plates lay a riddle drawn with a colored pencil.

"One of the gentlemen was a member of the Chevalier d'Aumont-Cléry, and—perhaps because he was of a Southern extraction—he was of a Southern race."

"Ah!" said I, astonished, "you mean to say that his name was James Borlsover?"

"Yes," said Librarian.

"Borlsovers?"

"Yes;—the same as yours."

```
gpt2.generate(sess,
              length=250,
              temperature=0.7,
              prefix="I handed it to the librarian in the loneliest
              of libraries and opened the volume.",
              nsamples=5,
              batch_size=5
              )
```

I handed it to the librarian in the loneliest of libraries and opened the volume.

It was the death's-head moth, a curious color, glittering, glossy, with shiny black wings. As I lifted the book from the librarian's clutches I saw that the front page had been rediscovered and was surrounded by a thick circle of red writing. The lower half of the book had evidently been misplaced and lay strewn on the floor, but the upper half was undiscovered and contained only the upper half of the death's-head moth. Curious! Curious!

"I wish I had a name for this curious sensation," I said, "one that means exactly what it expresses—'death's-head moth.' But I'm afraid I won't get any, and that's the end of the story."

I looked at the hand which had written the note. It clutched the book in both my two hands.

"Take it," said I, "or I'll yank it out of your hands, if you don't like it."

The hand dropped the book and retreated into the red writing.

"What in the world is this?" said I.

I handed it to the librarian in the loneliest of libraries and opened the volume.

It was the last volume in the series by Ronsard.

"I hate 'em!" I said, looking at my companion. "They're thieves and
assassins and messengers of death,
and enchanters of incalculable horrors. I hate 'em because they poison the well by covering it with books. I hate 'em because they steal books by false pretenses. I hate 'em because they ruin the reputations of innocent persons by telling lies about them in books. I
hate 'em because I know that they have books----"

"I know," said my friend, giving me another kiss, and turning the volume in my
hand.

"Books are the most treasured possession of any person," he said, looking at me with a smile.
"It is a mark of respect that he should wish to give me one of these days," I
said giving in.

Ronsard opened the book in his left hand and pointed to the photograph of Edward the Death's Head.

"That was some nasty dog," he said proudly.

"Yes, very nasty," said I, giving in.

"He

```
gpt2.generate(sess,
              length=250,
              temperature=1.2,
              prefix="I handed it to the librarian in the loneliest
              of libraries and opened the volume.",
              nsamples=5,
              batch_size=5
              )
```

I handed it to the librarian in the loneliest of libraries and opened the volume.

The old evangelist flipped through the pages in astonishment. All were bound together, the three great volumes of the Old Testimony. But the one page he read was so absurd that all his incredulity and fear shifted to the contrary.

It said simply: "These are the words of John the Baptist, which were found in the Harp of the Librarian of Kerselec: _I, John, searcheth and set in order by God's special will, which is somewhere between light and darkness, ascend not into the presence of my Father in the heavens, but into the presence of blasphemers, sorcerers, idolaters, and all liars."

That amusing passage, I fancy, escaped the notice of the wise men and the curious McCall and Co. As I pored over the matter they were, and can be seen in the upper crust of the new issue of Harper's Magazine.

This chamber is to be opened in the month of July, 1903. And, as I have said, the McCall and Company are immensely interested in ecclesiastical affairs, and I believe that the bit of information which I

```
gpt2.generate(sess,
              length=250,
              temperature=1.7,
              prefix="I handed it to the librarian in the loneliest
              of libraries and opened the volume.",
              nsamples=5,
              batch_size=5
              )
```

I handed it to the librarian in the loneliest of libraries and opened the volume.
Mr Hog erred first, picking it up three at a time, turning it
rather haphazardly among his numerous bookshelves. These records, too, were quickly obliterated. A moth, blue at first, quickly mounted on a manifold web, no doubt the spectral fingerprint of the beetle that was to definite destruction thousands of books down. Once you get a breeze kicked in your face, Duncan, unless you happen randomly into the life, property, or tears of an immortal string of books, I would have established a pernicious ghostly influence upon every one within six inches of me by now, depending upon it for protection. Whoever antsy themself here, seek it out—don't walk into its web!

That ellipsis matters, however briefly, Duncan. _I_ only warrant that those eighty-two numbered pages are out there somewhere. Key, lock, and frisk, they won't let me read them.

For at this time Manton escaped from me with an armored enthusiasm. Having carried him into the Brighton building after dinner one supple evening, weMovie No.
4006 Forsyth st.: By

```
gpt2.generate(sess,
              length=250,
              temperature=2,
              prefix="I handed it to the librarian in the loneliest
              of libraries and opened the volume.",
              nsamples=5,
              batch_size=5
              )
```

I handed it to the librarian in the loneliest of libraries and opened the volume. Several questions refused to die: What perform some fantastic ritual at Mamoun's temple? Who is here who in these columns by lord gasped at the rich thief? The investigation throwing light upon these ponderable arrangements attempted repeatedly to coaching cook. Gardening loads and partisan loads of tiny black matter pressed nFT toward me; I caught 'em ledge by grim cache

OVER

BY MR BURNELL
ST. AUGUSTIN MURRAY
666 Gazette Ltd., London.

January 1 northchild 404 HOWE TO BARYAGGLOGRAPH EVANGLE)Alex Ross was gone, inadequate for my reception, when £ Millionened Geoffrey fell fighting into my arms. Thirty-six hours since the libel did its cruel work, sty Summer work, the bones of my doomed joy converged on Jer Dangerfield Wood lest GEOFFERY JERSEY FINALITY BROTHER CORLEHR CAT THAT I NEVER WOULD WANTSPAWNTHESE WITHOUT INTERASTERAVERS GAME BOY ACROSS HOW ENTER AT LEAST SOME ARMIVEONE BECAUSE ST BUSISSOT EAR LIGED CROWNMC a genial aside, expressing my extreme dislike of lurking souls. How delightful to double dip myself in the absurd

ACKNOWLEDGEMENTS

This project would not have been possible without the support of the Isaac Newton Trust which provided funding for the 'Ghost Fictions' project, supporting a series of online workshops and the production of this booklet. The authors would like to thank all the participants in the CDH Learning 'Ghost Fictions' Guided Project and Methods Workshop October-December 2020 and the public workshop hosted by CRASSH in May 2021 for their contribution to the discussions which shaped the content of this work.

Jana Kleineberg's intricate design has created a beautiful artefact which we hope will stimulate debate, encourage reflection and prompt further creative exploration of the worlds of Automatic Literature.

www.ingramcontent.com/pod-product-compliance
Ingram Content Group UK Ltd.
Pitfield, Milton Keynes, MK11 3LW, UK
UKHW060020300726
14090UKWH00020B/1080